ENDANGERED ANIMALS

·········· DOT-TO-DOT ··········

Monica Russo

Sterling Publishing Co., Inc.   New York

This book is dedicated to the conservationists and field researchers who have worked hard on habitat preservation and who began the vital groundwork for the many successful breeding projects.

Acknowledgments

Technical data published by the Nature Conservancy, the International Council for Bird Preservation, and the offices of English Nature were vital in the preparation of this book. I am also grateful for fact sheets and other data provided by the Tennessee Valley Authority and many state, provincial, and independent wildlife organizations.

Meanings of Terms

Endangered:	Threatened with extinction.
Extinct:	Vanished. No survivors left on Earth.
Rare:	Very few survivors left on Earth.

10 9 8 7 6 5

Published 1994 by Sterling Publishing Company, Inc.
387 Park Avenue South, New York, N.Y. 10016
© 1994 by Monica Russo
Distributed in Canada by Sterling Publishing
% Canadian Manda Group, P.O. Box 920, Station U
Toronto, Ontario, Canada M8Z 5P9
Distributed in Great Britain and Europe by Cassell PLC
Villiers House, 41/47 Strand, London WC2N 5JE, England
Distributed in Australia by Capricorn Link (Australia) Pty Ltd.
P.O. Box 6651, Baulkham Hills, Business Centre, NSW 2153, Australia
Manufactured in the United States of America
All rights reserved

Sterling ISBN 0-8069-0520-4

About the Animals in This Book

All of the animals in this book need to be protected
in some way. Hunting, road construction, pesticide
pollution, and attacks by dogs and cats all cause
serious problems. *Very* few animal species become
rare today due to *natural* disasters, such as storms
or disease! No figures are given for the surviving
numbers of any animal, because these statistics can
change from month to month.

I have been fortunate to observe several of these
rare animals in their natural habitats. I hope that
all readers will have the opportunity to help protect
today's endangered creatures, and to observe them
in the wild also!

Monica Russo
Arundel, Maine
February, 1994

Name:	African Elephant
Size:	Up to 12 feet (3.6m) long, and about 10 to 13 feet (3–9m) high at the shoulder
Where It Is Endangered:	Africa
Habitat:	Plains, grasslands and scrublands

African Elephants were once quite common, and could be seen travelling in huge herds. But now, an older male with long tusks is a rare sight. The big tusks are really teeth, but they are only used for fighting or defending the young calves. Tusks can grow up to 10 feet (3m) long!

All elephants are vegetarians, eating leaves, grass and tree branches. A large elephant may need as much as 300 pounds of food each day.

The greatest enemy of the African Elephant is man—hunters and ivory poachers have killed thousands of these majestic animals. Many elephants now live in parks and reserves, where they can be protected.

Brownish black, or dark grey

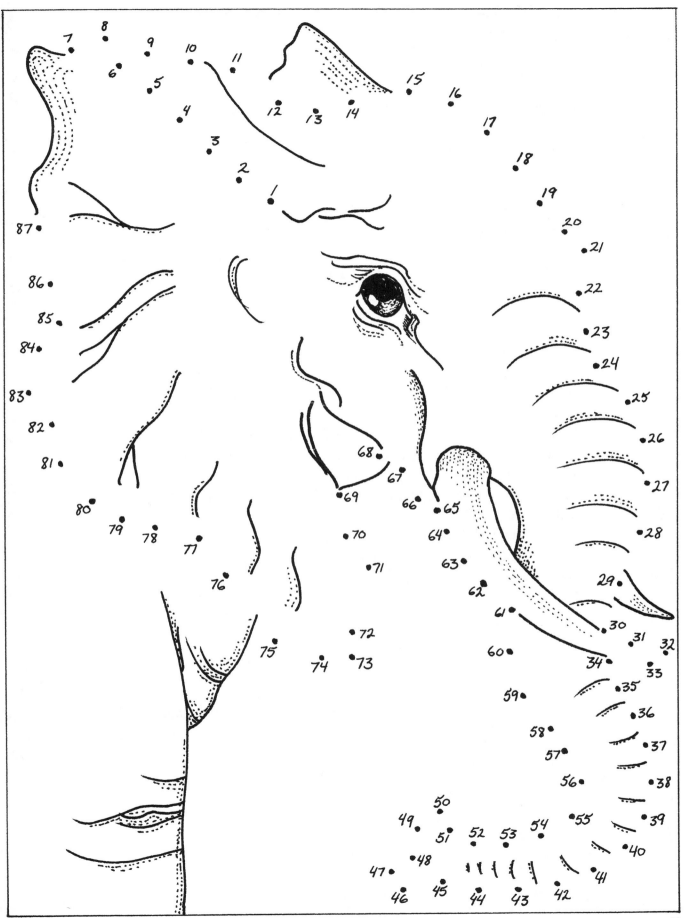

Name:	Arabian Oryx
Size:	About 3 feet (1m) high at the shoulder
Where It Is Endangered:	Yemen, in the Middle East
Habitat:	Open scrubby plains at the edge of the desert

The beautiful Oryx is a type of small antelope. Its graceful horns are about two feet (.6m) long.

It is already extinct as a wild animal! Hunters have killed off every single wild Arabian Oryx. But some zoos and parks have kept the Oryx in captivity, and many of these animals have been born and raised in those zoos. Those young Oryxes are now being released into their natural habitat. Some oryxes born in zoos have been flown back by plane to their desert homes to start new herds again. Now these animals will have to be carefully protected.

Very light tan (almost white) body, chocolate-brown legs, brown patch on face

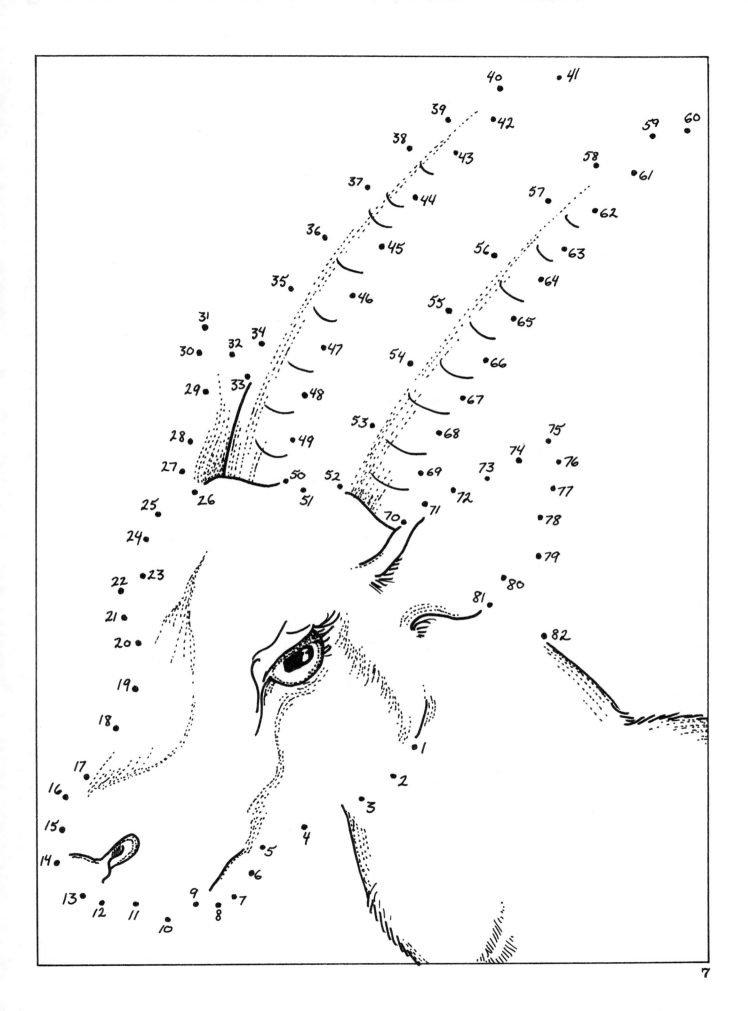

Name:	Baiji Dolphin
Size:	About 7 feet (2.1m) long
Where It Is Endangered:	China
Habitat:	Yangtze River

Dolphins are mammals—not fish! They are related to whales and orcas. Most dolphins around the world live in the ocean, and very few live in rivers.

The Baiji Dolphin has a very long nose, or "beak." It eats mostly fish. This rare dolphin may be on the verge of extinction. The Yangtze River is very muddy and polluted, and the dolphins have a hard time finding fish to eat. They are disturbed by the noise of boat motors and injured by fishhooks and propeller blades.

A Chinese conservation group is trying to save Baiji Dolphins by keeping some of them in a protected channel, where they will be safe. But a construction project to build a dam may now spell disaster for the remaining dolphins!

Grey above, white underneath

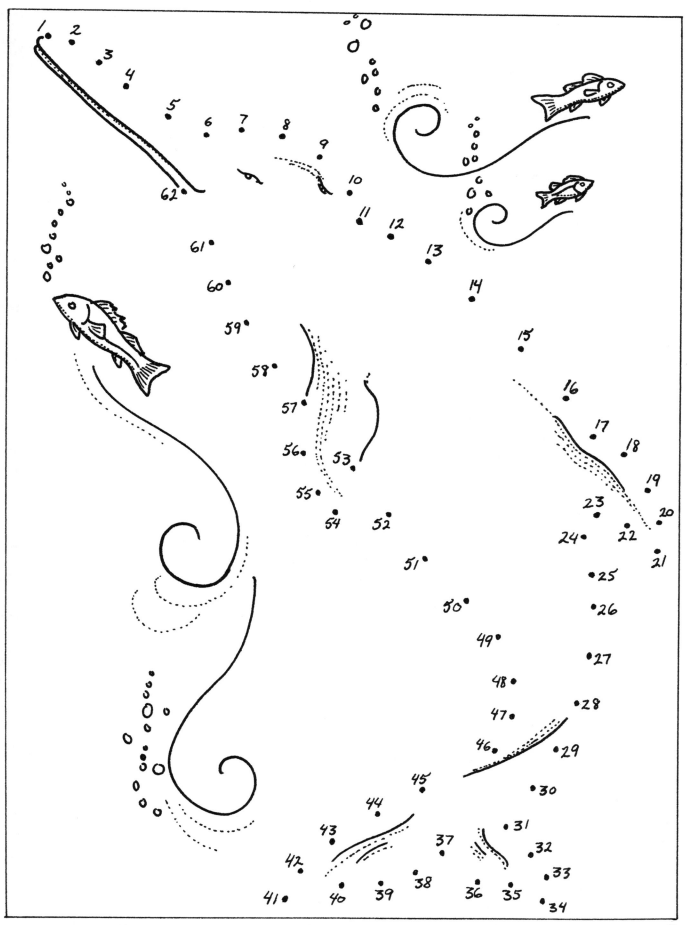

Name:	Bald Eagle
Size:	About 35 inches (1m) long Wingspan: 6 to 8 feet (1.8–2.4m) across
Where It Is Endangered:	United States
Habitat:	Forests near lakes, coastal bays or rivers

The Bald Eagle is the national bird of the United States, and it is protected by federal laws. This eagle grows white head feathers when it's about five years old. Until then, it has dark brown head feathers. The Bald Eagle uses its strong curved claws and beak to catch fish.

Pesticides like DDT have killed many Bald Eagles and prevented their eggs from hatching. Human activity at nesting areas can cause the parent eagles to leave, or not lay eggs.

Snowy white head, yellow beak, yellow eyes. Body feathers are chocolate-brown.

Name:	Bengal Tiger
Size:	About 6 feet (1.8m) long, with a tail about 3 feet (1m) long.
Where It Is Endangered:	India
Habitat:	Jungle forests and grassy fields

The Bengal Tiger is a member of the cat family. Its relatives include the African lion, ocelot, lynx and jaguar.

A fierce hunter, the tiger attacks and kills other animals in the jungle. An adult Bengal Tiger weighs about 500 pounds (225 kg). The wavy stripes on its fur are good camouflage, helping to hide it when it hunts in tall grasses.

The Bengal Tiger is very endangered, and its population keeps declining. Hunters have killed many of these beautiful animals.

Yellow-tan, with black stripes

Name:	Black-Footed Ferret
Size:	About 2 feet (.6m) long
Where It Is Endangered:	Western United States
Habitat:	Prairie grasslands and plains

Ferrets are members of the weasel family, along with skunks and minks. At one time, there were many Black-Footed Ferrets, but now they are rare. Ferrets hunt and eat prairie dogs, which are rodents. The ferrets live in the same areas that prairie dogs live in, and use old prairie dog burrows for their own dens. Prairie dogs were once poisoned in great numbers because they were a nuisance to farmers. Some conservationists believe the poisons might have killed a lot of the Black-Footed Ferrets, too.

Note: Some ferrets sold as pets in pet stores look just like these rare animals, but they are not wild Black-Footed Ferrets!

Yellow-buff body, black mask across face, black feet, black tail-tip

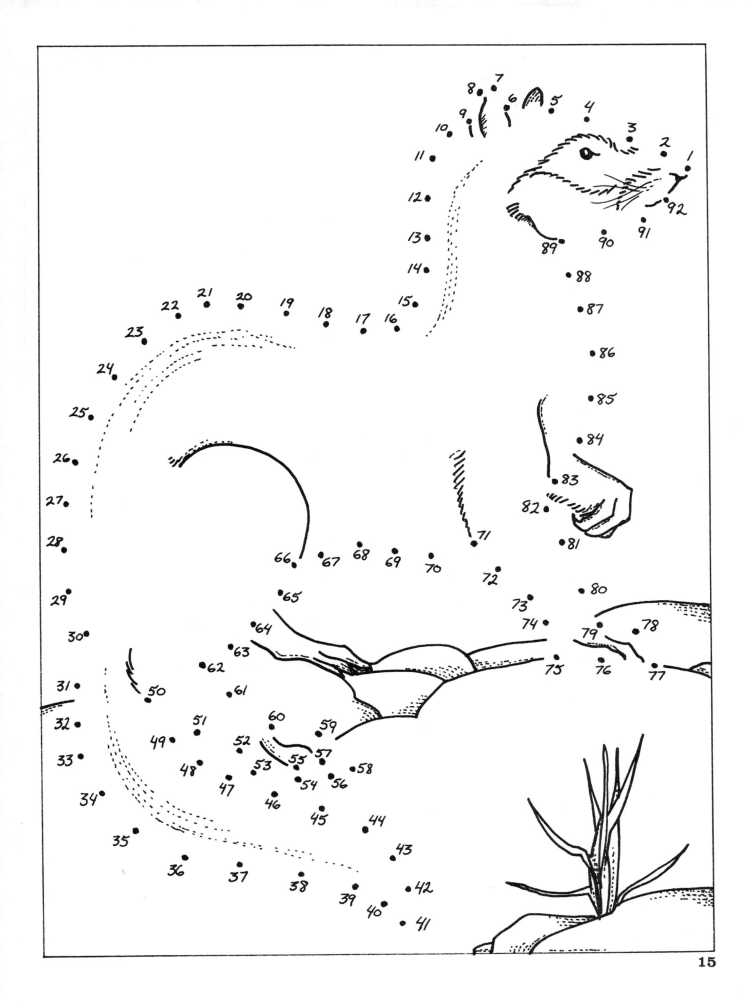

Name:	Blue Whale
Size:	About 80 feet (24m) long Record size is about 100 feet (30m) long!
Where It Is Endangered:	All oceans
Habitat:	Oceans, coastal bays and gulfs.

A Blue Whale can dive close to 1,000 feet (300m) deep. A newborn whale is just over 20 feet (6m) long.

Blue Whales don't have teeth. Instead, they have "sifters" called baleen plates, which strain out tiny shrimp-like creatures that the whales eat. The water drains away from the baleen strainers, leaving the whale with a mouthful of food! Thousands of these huge whales were once killed for their oil, but now they are on the U.S. endangered species list and are protected by law.

Dark blue-grey, lighter spots or blotches on the side

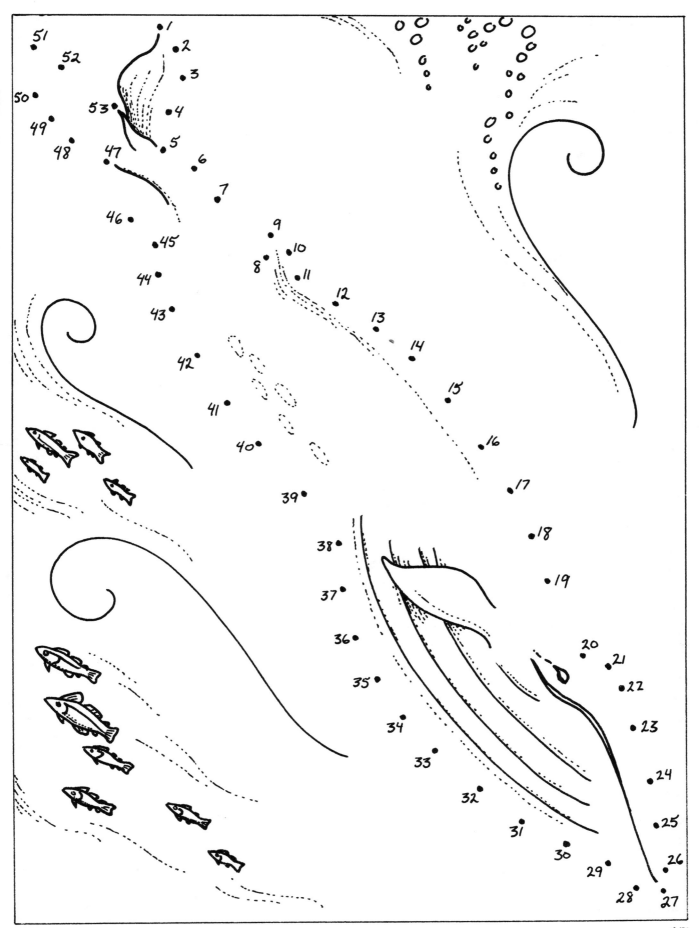

Name:	California Condor
Size:	Wingspan: About 9 to 10 feet (2.7–3m) across (more than twice the span of your outstretched arms!)
Where It Is Endangered:	Southern California, U.S.
Habitat:	Mountains and open grasslands

This huge bird may have an ugly face, but it is magnificent in flight, soaring, gliding and swooping high in the mountains. Condors are scavengers, feeding only on dead animals. But they like to be clean, taking baths in mountain pools and streams!

There are very few Condors left, and most of them are in zoos. The Condor is endangered, because many have been shot by hunters or poisoned, or their nesting sites have been disturbed. Condors only lay one or two eggs—every *other* year!

Shining black feathers, pinkish red neck, yellowish head, red eyes, long silky black feathers around the neck

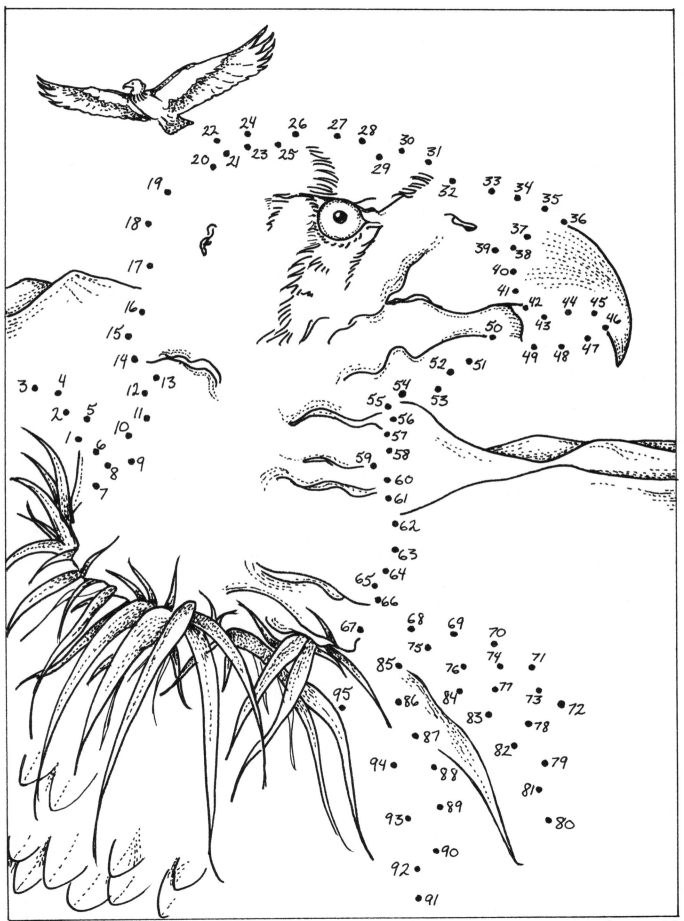

Name:	Cheetah
Size:	About 7 feet (2.1m) long, including the tail
Where It Is Endangered:	Africa, Mideast, India
Habitat:	Open grassy plains

Cheetahs are swift and slender hunters. They eat birds, small animals and larger animals like gazelles. They can run as fast as 75 miles per hour, for a short dash.

Cheetahs once lived in India, but they are probably extinct there now. No one has seen wild Cheetahs in India for a long time. Some Cheetahs are left in Afghanistan, Iran and Egypt. Cheetahs in Africa live in protected reserves and parks. It's especially important to protect the Cheetahs in Africa, because that's where the largest population remains.

Tan or light yellowish brown, black circles and spots

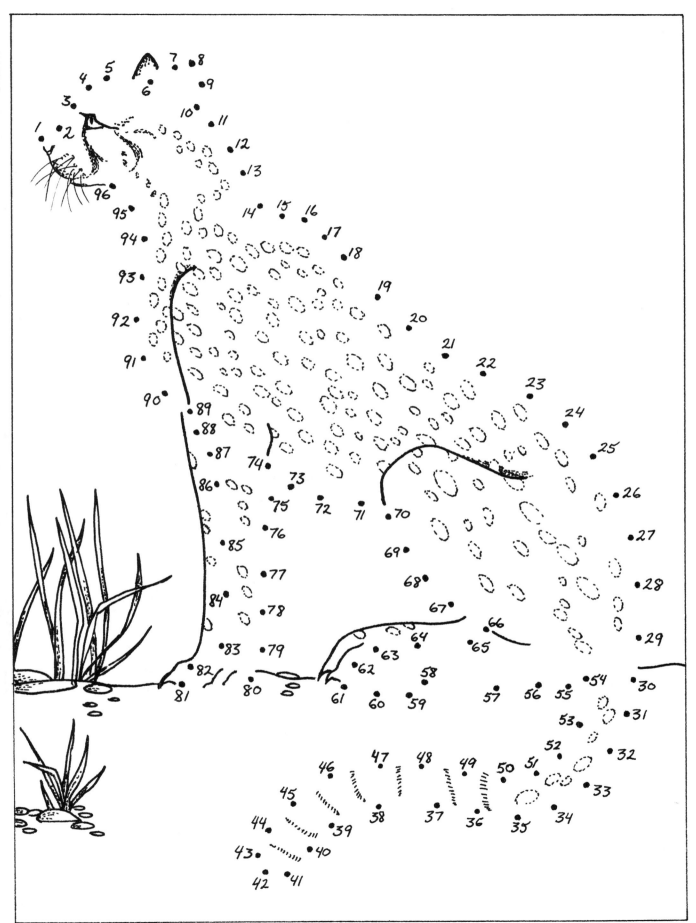

21

Name:	Desert Tortoise
Size:	Up to 14 inches (35cm) long
Where It Is Endangered:	Southwestern United States
Habitat:	Sandy and grassy desert areas

A Desert Tortoise is a very slow animal. It has strong feet and claws, and it digs burrows into the desert sand. It crawls into the burrows to get away from the sun and heat.

This reptile lives in the hot, dry desert of the American Southwest. There is very little rainfall, so the Desert Tortoise has to get its moisture from the plants it eats. The Desert Tortoise eats grasses, leaves and fruit. If no rain falls at all, there may be no green plants to eat, and the Tortoise may starve.

Brown, lighter yellowish brown patches on the shell. The cactus flowers are bright yellow.

Name:	Finback Whale
Size:	Up to 75 feet (22.5m) long
Where It Is Endangered:	Atlantic and Pacific oceans
Habitat:	Oceans and large coastal bays

This mammal is also called the Fin Whale. It has a small fin on its back, towards the tail. Like other whales, the Finback eats fish and krill, which are tiny shrimp. Female Finbacks are longer than males. They have only one calf every other year.

The Finback has been hunted for many years for its meat, and for oil from its fat. Too much hunting has caused this whale to decline in population (along with the Blue Whale and the Humpback Whale.) The Finback is now on the U.S. endangered species list.

Dark grey-black above, white or light grey underneath. Some Finbacks have yellowish sides.

25

Name:	Golden Lion Tamarin
Size:	About the size of a squirrel
Where It Is Endangered:	Brazil
Habitat:	Jungle forests

Golden Lion Tamarins are small monkeys, named for their lion-like manes. They have pointed ears, long tails, and five fingers on their hands, like other monkeys. Tamarins eat fruit, seeds and insects.

Some Tamarins have been raised in zoos so they can be released back into the jungle. Scientists are hoping these captive-raised Tamarins will survive in the wild.

Another species of Tamarin, called the Cotton Top because of its white mane, is endangered in Colombia.

Orange-brown or golden brown fur

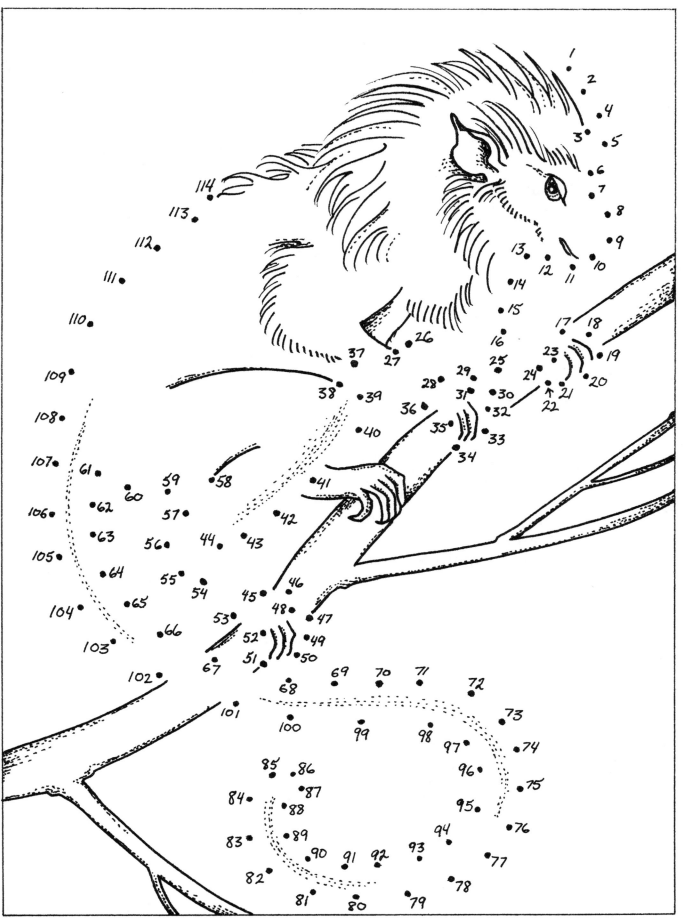

Name:	Golden Toad
Size:	Almost 2 inches (5cm) long
Where It Is Endangered:	Costa Rica
Habitat:	Cloud forests and rain forests

All toads are amphibians—animals that can live in both land and water. Like other toads, Golden Toads eat insects.

Male Golden Toads are bright orange, but females are mostly green and black. Males gather together in groups to sing for mates, but only a few males have been found in the past few years. Once there were thousands, but now they are rare. The populations of toads from other parts of the world are decreasing also, so scientists are very concerned.

Bright orange-gold

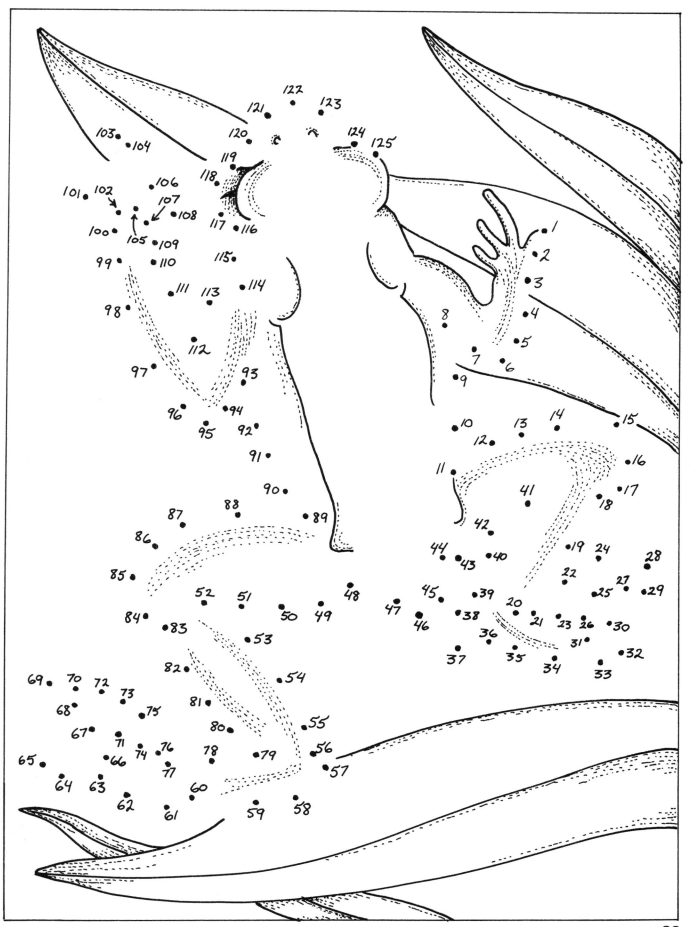

Name:	Gorgone Checkerspot
Size:	Wingspan: Less than 2 inches (5cm) across
Where It Is Endangered:	Illinois
Habitat:	Prairie fields and grassy meadows

This small butterfly is getting a great amount of attention! It has been found in many parts of the United States, but it is never very common. Conservationists are trying to start new populations in Illinois by bringing in Checkerspots from other areas.

All butterflies start out as caterpillars. The caterpillar of the Gorgone Checkerspot eats the leaves of asters and sunflowers.

The Gorgone Checkerspot is endangered because its home is often destroyed. When a field is mown or a road is built through a meadow, the habitat is ruined.

Orange and gold with black near the edge of the wing

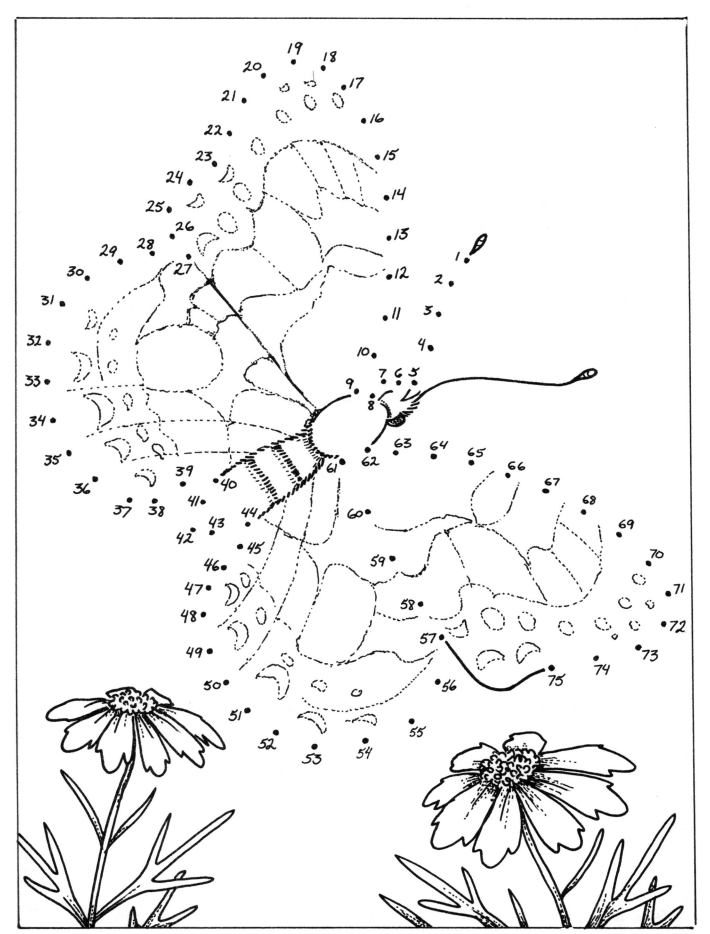

Name:	Grizzly Bear
Size:	Up to 8 feet (2.4m) long
Where It Is Endangered:	North America
Habitat:	Rocky Mountain forests

The Grizzly Bear is a huge, ferocious animal. It eats fruits, berries and smaller animals, and it can even kill deer and the young calves of moose. It has strong, sharp claws that it uses to catch fish right out of a river.

The Grizzly has very thick fur. Because the tips of the hairs are white, the fur has a silvery, frosted look.

In the United States, most Grizzlies live in Yellowstone National Park, and many cubs have been born there. Some of the bears have had collars with radio transmitters put on them, so scientists can track them by radio.

Golden brown

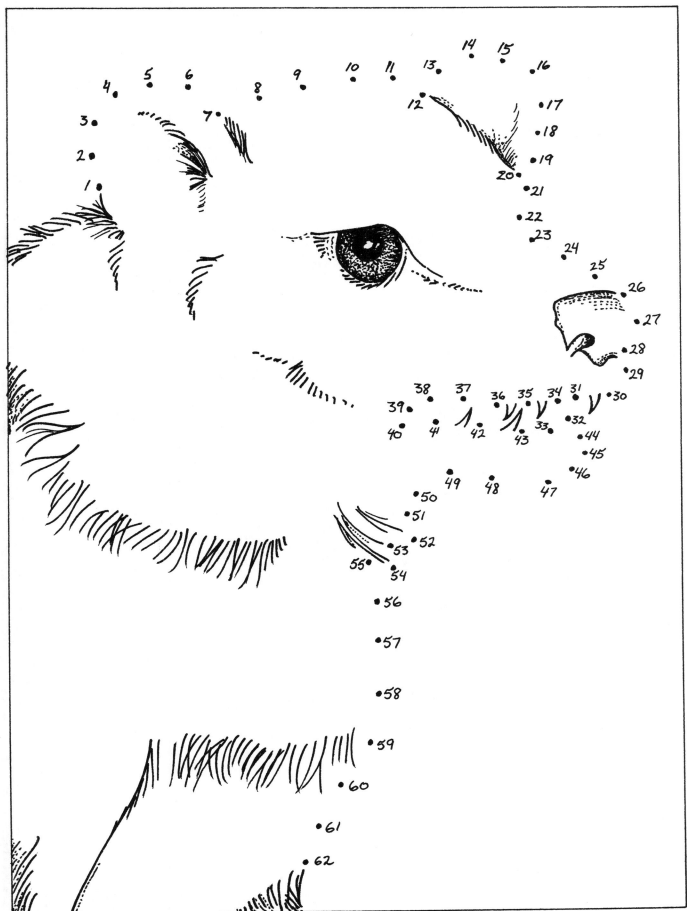

Name:	Hawaiian Monk Seal
Size:	About 7 feet (2.1m) long
Where It Is Endangered:	The leeward island chain of the Hawaiian Islands
Habitat:	Shallow water, near small islands

All seals can swim and dive well, using their strong flippers. They don't spend all their time in the ocean, but come onto shore to rest and to sun themselves. Like other species of seals, Monk Seals eat fish. Young seals are called pups.

Seals around the world have been hunted for their meat and fur, so many species are now protected by law. Some seals become injured when they get tangled in discarded plastic ropes and nets. Two other Monk Seals are endangered also: the Caribbean Monk Seal and the Mediterranean Monk Seal.

Silver-grey above, white underneath

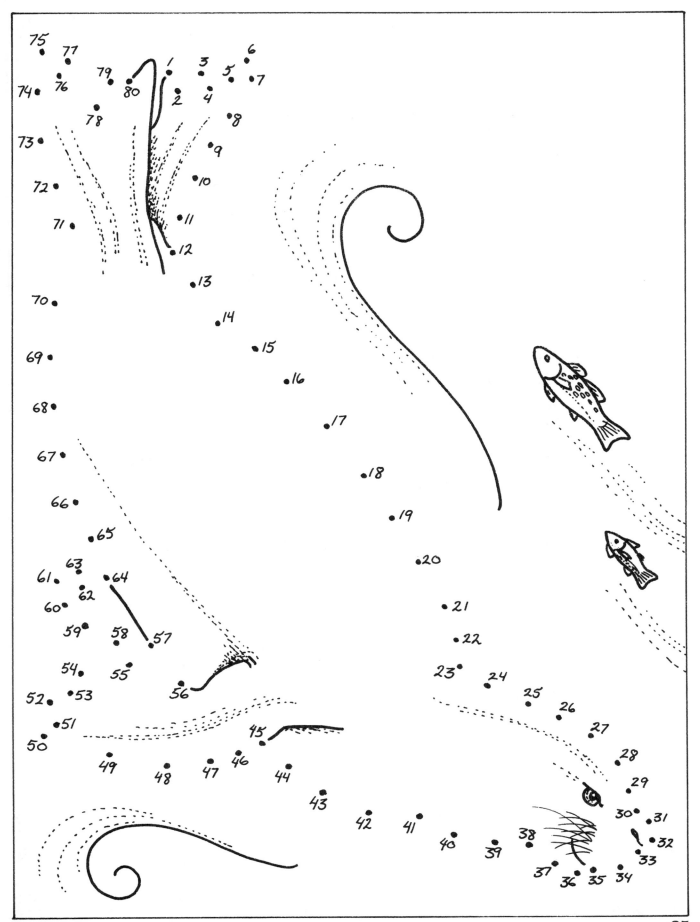

Name:	Honeycreeper
Size:	About 5 inches (12.5cm) long
Where It Is Endangered:	Island of Hawaii
Habitat:	Mountain forests

The Hawaiian name for this little bird is 'Akiapola'au (pronounced a-kee-a-po-lay-ow). Its song is a warbling, trilling whistle. It has a slender curved beak that it uses to hunt insects.

The Honeycreeper is now rare because pigs, goats and sheep have uprooted and grazed the forest plants where it lives. There are several types of Honeycreepers and a few are already extinct, so it is important to save the habitat of the 'Akiapola'au.

Olive-green above, yellowish underneath

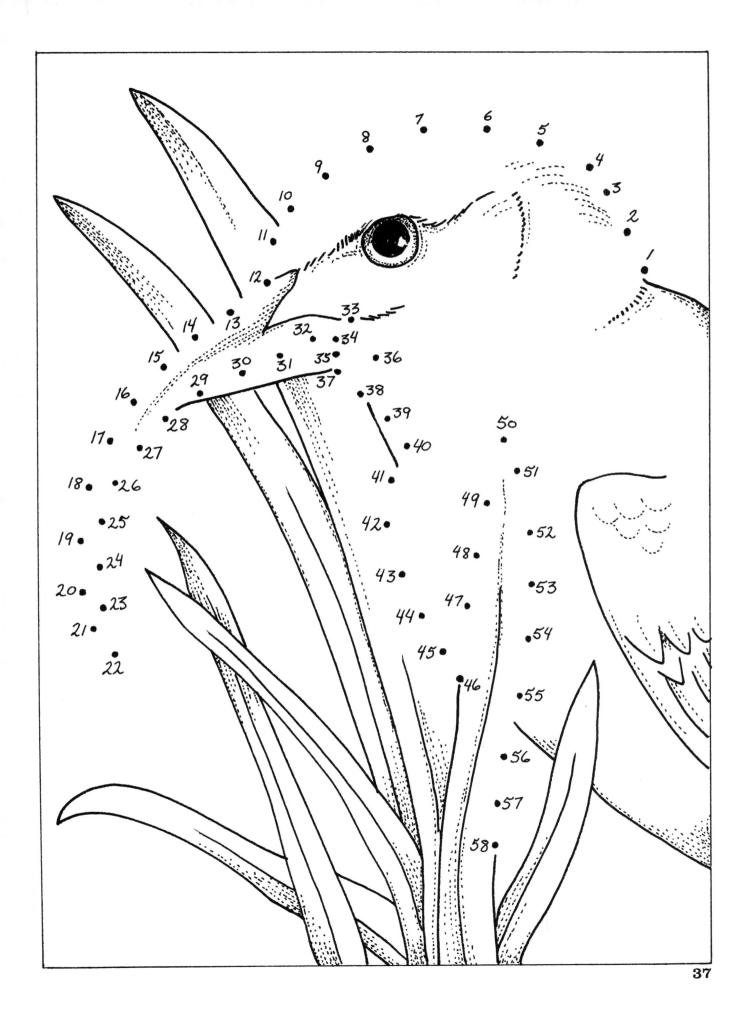

Name:	Ivory-Billed Woodpecker
Size:	About 18 to 20 inches (45—50cm) long
Where It Is Endangered:	Southeastern U.S.
Habitat:	Old swamp forests with dead trees

This beautiful crow-sized woodpecker uses its long beak to chisel away bark and wood to hunt for insects. But it may already be extinct in the United States! No one has seen it for many years. It may have become rare because forest trees have been cut down for lumber or to make fields for soybeans. Only a few pairs of closely related woodpeckers now live in Cuba. Scientists hope that these remaining birds can be protected successfully.

Bright red crest, glossy black body feathers, yellow eyes, white beak, white stripe on neck, white wing patches

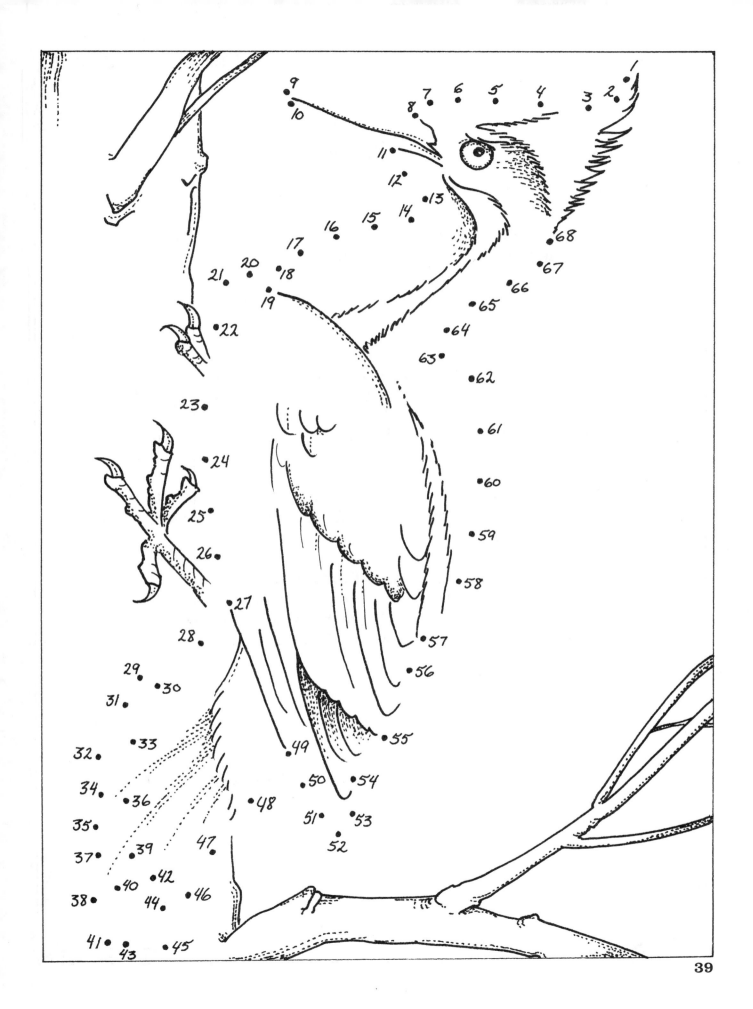

Name:	Kakapo
Size:	About 2 feet (.6m) long
Where It Is Endangered:	New Zealand, and nearby islands
Habitat:	Old forests and scrublands

The Kakapo (pronounced kak-a-PO) is a type of parrot, sometimes called the Owl Parrot, because of its large round face. It has very small wings and can't really fly much—but it can glide a little if it has to.

Male Kakapos use a deep, booming call to attract mates. These plump, greenish parrots eat berries, leaves, fruit and seeds.

This bird is on the verge of extinction. Many Kakapos have been killed by dogs and cats. Very few are left, so some of them have been taken to small islands where they might be protected more easily.

Mossy green and greenish brown

Name:	Key Deer
Size:	Less than 4 feet (1.2m) high at the shoulder
Where It Is Endangered:	Florida
Habitat:	Small islands (the "Keys") near the coast of Florida

These small deer used to live on a chain of islands, swimming from one island to another. Now they are very rare and mostly confined to one island. Key Deer can run and jump swiftly and gracefully. Like other North American deer, they are vegetarians. They eat leaves, buds, twigs and grass. Male Key Deer have antlers. When the antlers are new, they are covered with a soft fuzz called "velvet."

Some Key Deer have been killed by hunters and by speeding cars. The destruction of their habitat is also a big problem. When new roads are constructed, for example, the deer lose their feeding areas and shelter. Then they become homeless and cannot survive.

Light brown, with a black band around their nose

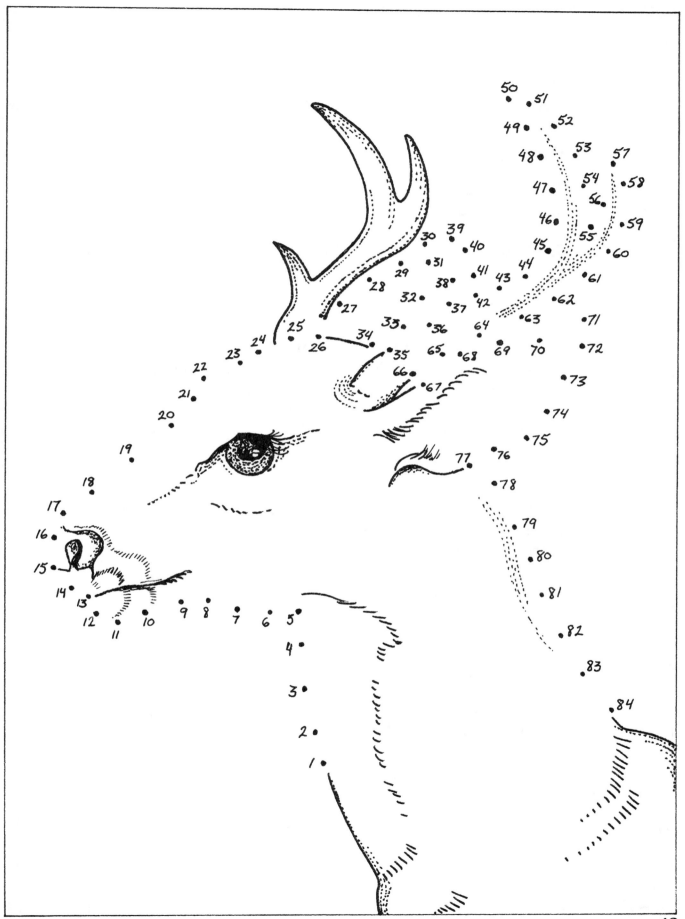

Name:	Kiwi
Size:	About 2 feet (.6m) long
Where It Is Endangered:	New Zealand
Habitat:	Pine forests with ferns

Kiwis are birds—but they can't fly. Their wings are much too small. All Kiwis have long thin beaks and strong legs. Their feathers are so thin and fine that they look like fur instead of feathers. Kiwis eat worms, insects and fruit, and are usually active at night.

Several different species of Kiwi live in New Zealand and Australia. In New Zealand, the Little Spotted Kiwi and the Brown Kiwi are protected. Protection is important: In one New Zealand sanctuary, more than a dozen Brown Kiwis were killed by just one dog!

This Kiwi is dark brown.

Name:	Koala
Size:	About 2 feet (.6m) tall
Where It Is Endangered:	Australia
Habitat:	Eucalyptus forests

This charming animal with hairy ears and a big nose is sometimes called a Koala Bear. But it isn't a bear at all, and it isn't even related to bears!

In Australia, the Koala is sometimes called the koolewong or the narnagoon, names given to it by the native Aborigines.

Koalas are great tree climbers. They eat only the leaves of eucalyptus trees. Zoos and wildlife parks that keep Koalas must have a steady supply of eucalyptus leaves to keep the Koalas healthy. There used to be millions of Koalas, but disease, hunting, and the cutting down of forests have decreased their population severely.

Golden brown or ash-brown fur, brownish black nose

47

Name:	Komodo Dragon
Size:	Up to 10 or 12 feet (3–3.6m) long
Where It Is Endangered:	Indonesia (Komodo Island and Rinca)
Habitat:	Island forests

The Komodo Dragon is the largest lizard in the world! Most Dragons live in a protected park on Komodo Island. They hunt for food during the day and spend nights in burrows in the ground. These huge reptiles kill and eat wild pigs and other small animals.

Protecting a rare animal like the Komodo Dragon can be difficult, because many people don't care about saving animals that are ugly or frightening. But wildlife workers at the Smithsonian's National Zoological Park have successfully hatched several young Dragons from eggs.

Black and brown. Young Komodo Dragons have lighter bands

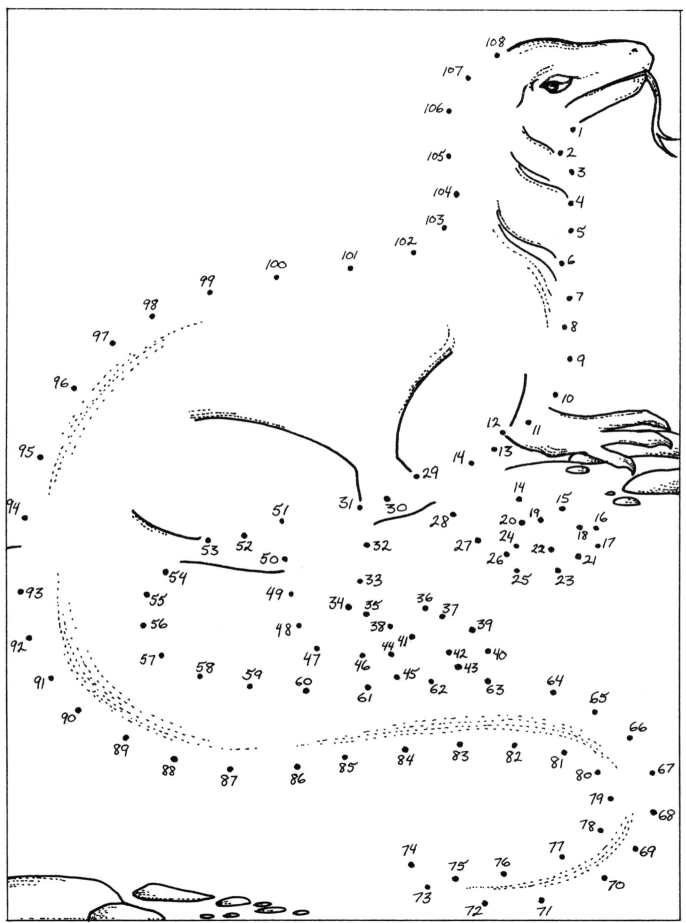

Name:	Large Blue
Size:	Wingspan: Less than 1½ inches (3.75m) across
Where It Is Endangered:	England
Habitat:	Open grassy slopes, with thyme plants

This beautiful blue butterfly is already extinct in England! It may have disappeared because its habitat of open fields has changed over time—many fields and meadows have become overgrown, and some fields have been ploughed or grazed over. All butterflies develop from caterpillars. The caterpillar of the Large Blue feeds on thyme. After it eats this plant, it crawls into a nest of red ants, where it eats the young grubs of the ants!

Caterpillars of Large Blues from Scandinavia have been brought to England, in hopes of starting new colonies. Once the caterpillars become butterflies, scientists hope they will stay in England.

Blue, darker blue border, dark blue-black spots on the front wings

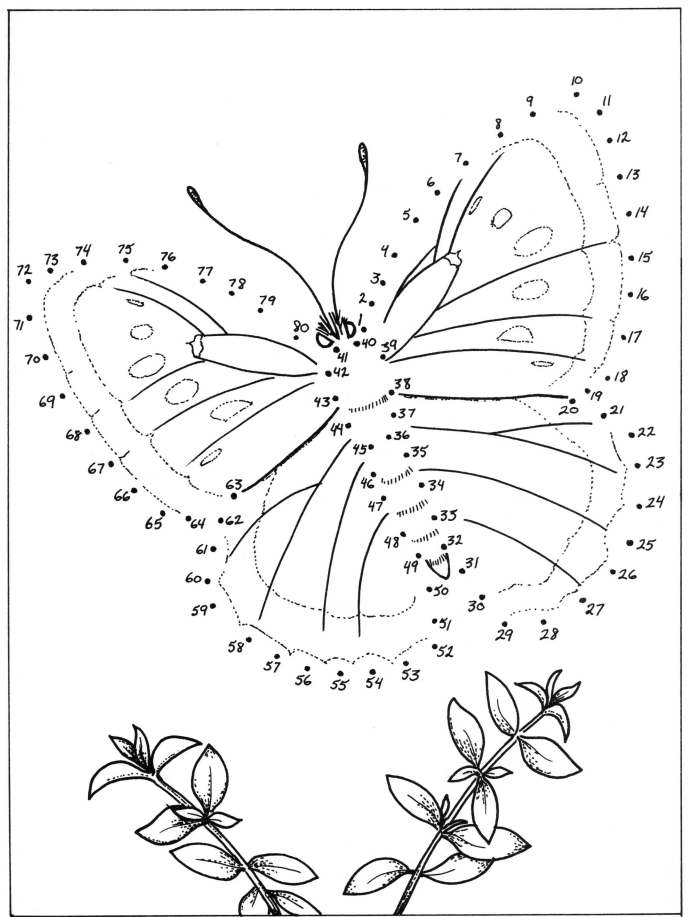

Name:	Leatherback Turtle
Size:	About 8 feet (2.4m) long
Where It Is Endangered:	Atlantic and Pacific oceans
Habitat:	Deep oceans

The Leatherback is the largest sea turtle in the world! It is named for its tough leathery back, which has seven bumpy ridges. Most other turtles have an upper shell made of hard, bony plates.

Female Leatherbacks come to shore only when they lay eggs. A few known nesting sites are on the beaches of Costa Rica and St. Croix in the Virgin Islands. As soon as the baby turtles hatch, they head right down to the waves, like the little Leatherback on the next page.

Leatherbacks eat jellyfish. Some of them are killed when they try to eat plastic bags that have been thrown into the ocean—probably because the bags look like jellyfish floating in the water.

Dark brownish black, speckled all over with white

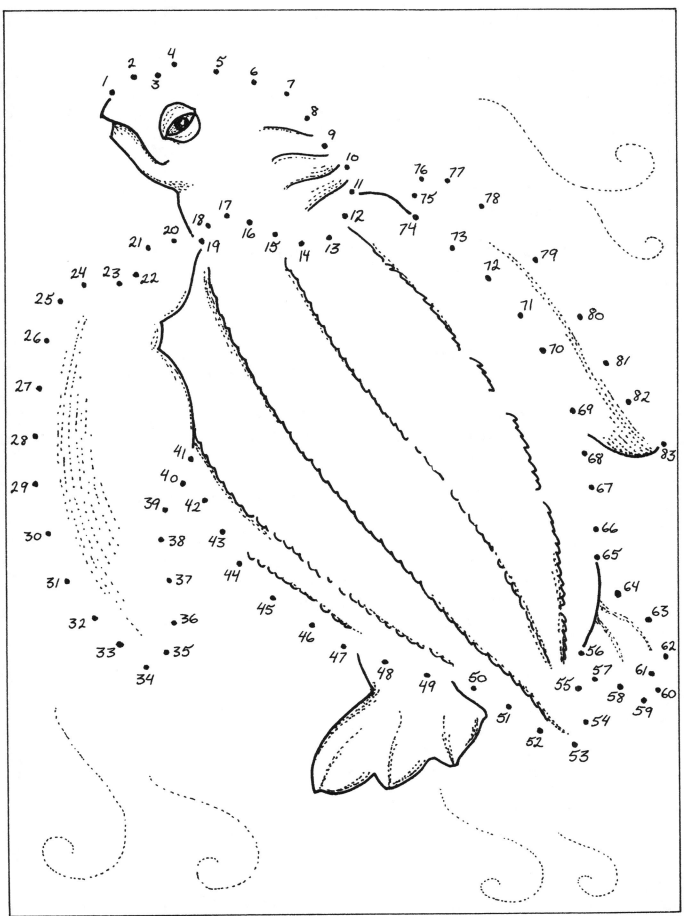

Name:	Panda
Size:	About 6 feet (1.8m) long
Where It Is Endangered:	Southwest China
Habitat:	Cold bamboo forests and mountains

Pandas are sometimes called Panda Bears, but they are not related to bears at all. The Panda's favorite foods include bamboo leaves and stems, fruit and berries. It also eats other plants and meat. A large full-grown Panda can eat as much as 40 pounds (18 kg) of bamboo in one day.

Many Pandas have been killed by hunters for their beautiful fur. Now people are very interested in protecting the Panda. Some zoos and wildlife parks have been successful in breeding Pandas, and some baby Pandas have been born in captivity. Conservationists hope this will keep the Panda from becoming extinct.

Snow-white head, black ears, a black spot around each eye, black legs and shoulders

Name:	Peregrine Falcon
Size:	Up to 20 inches (50cm) long Wingspan: to 40 inches (100cm) across
Where It Is Endangered:	North America, Europe—especially Great Britain and Scandinavia—the Mideast
Habitat:	Open country, tundra and mountains nearly worldwide

This bird of prey nests on cliffs, mountain ledges and even city buildings. Swift and graceful, it feeds mostly on other birds, diving to strike its prey at speeds of 200 miles (320km) per hour!

The Peregrine Falcon is now protected by federal law in the United States. Widespread use of the pesticide DDT killed many Peregrines and prevented their eggs from hatching.

Conservationists and falconers (people who hunt with trained falcons) have worked together to breed and hatch Peregrines in captivity. They also work hard to protect the nesting sites of wild Peregrines from human interference.

Black head feathers, slate-grey back, white chest

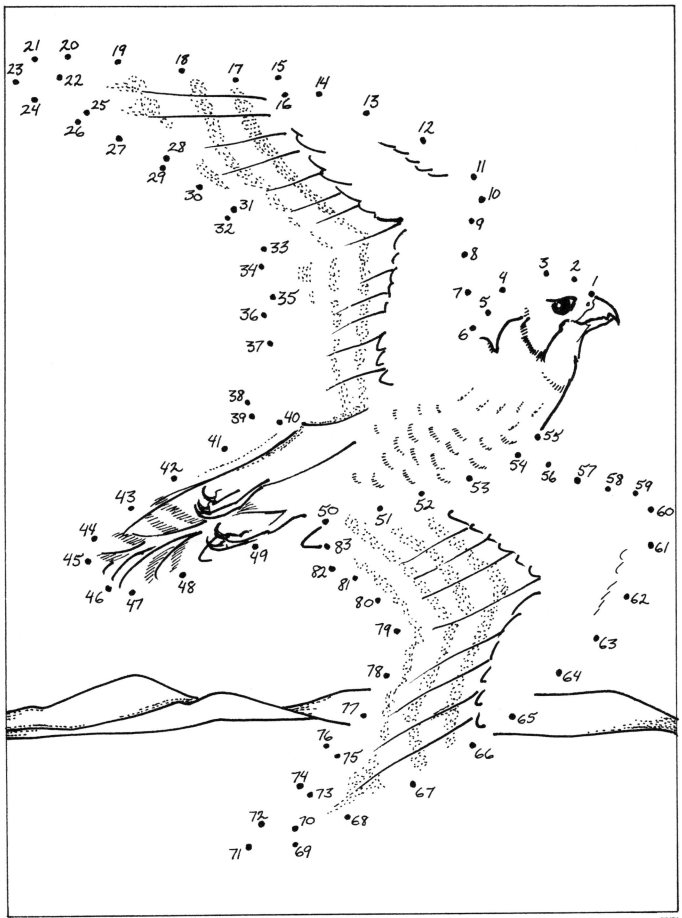

Name:	Philippine Eagle
Size:	Up to 40 inches (100cm) long
Where It Is Endangered:	Island of Mindinao, Philippines
Habitat:	Deep forests

The Philippine Eagle is larger than the Bald Eagle of North America. It has a large, curved beak, strong feet and sharp talons. This beautiful bird of prey feeds on monkeys, squirrels and lemurs in the forest. Its crest feathers are long and graceful.

Males and females look alike, and mated pairs remain together for life.

Some Philippine Eagles are now kept in captivity, where scientists hope they can breed and lay eggs in safety. Many eagles have been shot by hunters, and their nesting habitat is being destroyed as trees are cut for lumber.

Slate-grey beak, gold-brown crest, white chest, brown body

Name:	Pine Barrens Tree Frog
Size:	Less than 2 inches (5cm) long
Where It Is Endangered:	New Jersey, U.S.
Habitat:	Bogs, swamps and ponds

This colorful little frog eats small insects. It has long toes that help it climb around on leaves and twigs. It always likes to be near water.

The Pine Barrens Tree frog was once common, but now it is an endangered species in New Jersey. Scientists aren't sure why this frog has become so rare, but pollution in ponds may be one harmful cause. Destruction of swampy areas may also be part of the problem.

Bright, light green—like the color of green apples. The sides of its belly and legs are lavender.

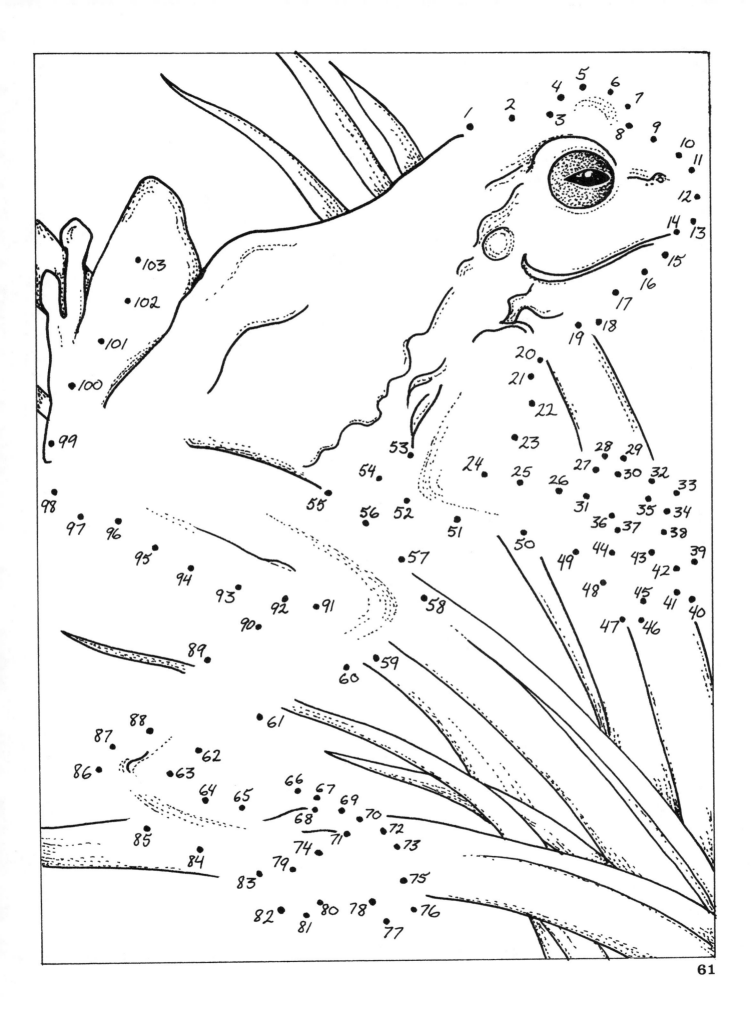

Name:	Piping Plover
Size:	About 5 to 6 inches (12.5—15cm) long
Where It Is Endangered:	North America
Habitat:	Bays, inlets, beaches, sand dunes, shorelines

This ghostly pale shorebird is named for its high-pitched, piping call. Its back is the same color as the sandy beach, so it's almost invisible when it runs on the sand dunes. Piping Plovers nest right on the sand, but people and dogs using the beach sometimes prevent it from nesting successfully.

This little bird is now protected by law in the United States. Wildlife workers and park rangers put up fences to protect the Plover's nests, but this makes some people very angry. They can't play on the beach when the baby Plovers have hatched, and the beach is fenced off.

Sandy tan above, yellow beak, black collar and forehead, white chest

Name:	Red Squirrel
Size:	About 16 inches (40 cm) long
Where It Is Endangered:	England
Habitat:	Forests and woodlands

This small squirrel has long, tufted ears. It eats pine seeds, beech nuts, hazel nuts, acorns, mushrooms and berries. Red Squirrels build dens of leaves in trees, or live in hollow trunks. They don't need to hibernate all winter, but they will stay in their dens during a spell of bad winter weather.

Red Squirrels are rare because the larger Grey Squirrels have taken over much of their habitat. Grey Squirrels were brought to England from America. Wildlife workers have set up feeding stations for the Red Squirrels, which the bigger Grey Squirrels can't get into.

Note: The Red Squirrel of North America is a different species, and is not endangered.

Reddish brown, white underneath. Their fur is more grey in the winter than at other times of year.

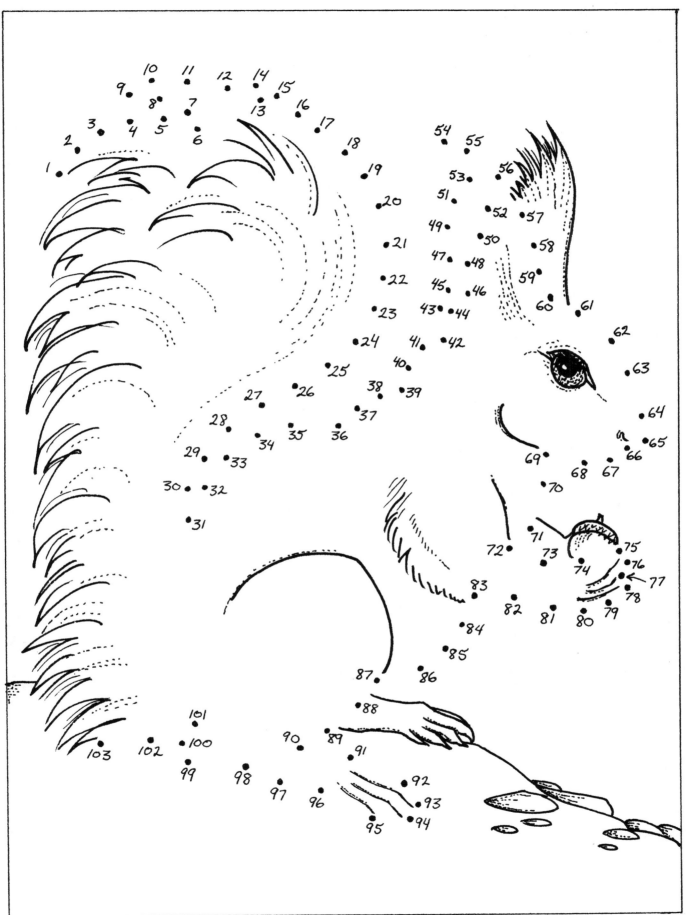

Name:	Resplendent Quetzal
Size:	About 3 to 4 feet (.9–1.2m) long, including the long tail
Where It Is Endangered:	Mexico to Panama
Habitat:	Rain forest, dense jungle forests

This Quetzal (pronounced ket-SAL) is the national bird of Guatemala. Only the male Quetzal has beautiful long tail feathers. These splendid birds nest in hollow trees, and they eat fruit.

In some areas of Mexico and Costa Rica this Quetzal is extremely rare. Tropical rain forests are being destroyed to make coffee farms and ranches, so the Quetzal's habitat is disappearing!

Green head, neck, back and tail feathers, bright red belly, yellow beak

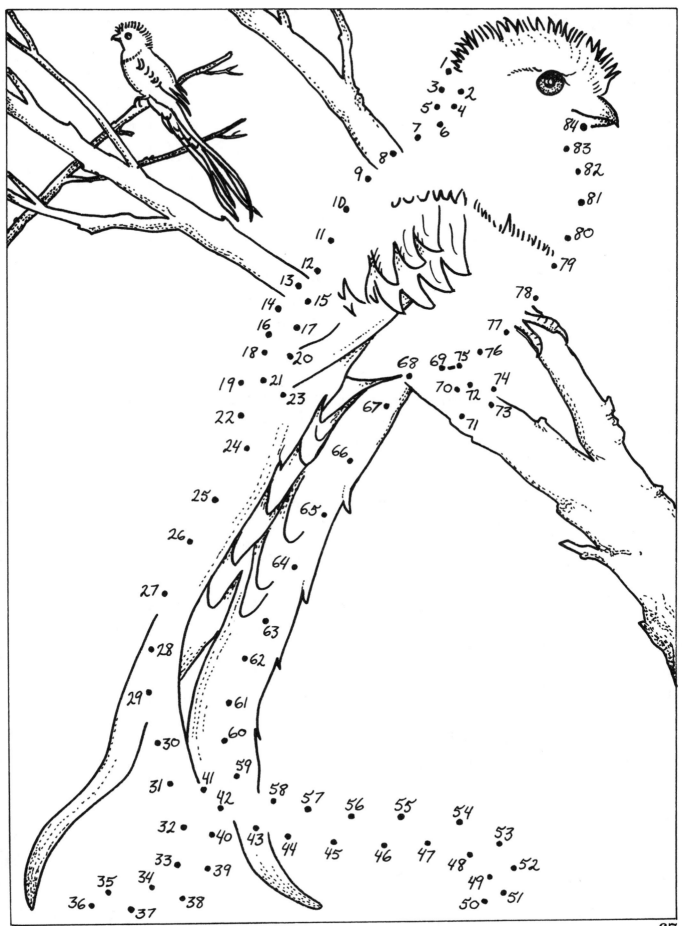

Name:	Snail Darter
Size:	About 3 inches (7.5cm) long
Where It Is Endangered:	Tennessee, U.S.
Habitat:	Freshwater lakes and streams with gravel bottoms

There are many different kinds of Darters in the United States, but the Snail Darter only lives in one small area. It got its name because it likes to eat snails!

A small fish, it has caused some big concerns in the American southeast. An important dam-building project had to be delayed until conservationists could learn more about the Darter.

The Snail Darter isn't the only rare fish in North America. There are species of Sturgeon and Trout that also need protection.

Reddish brown, darker brown bands on back, yellowish underneath

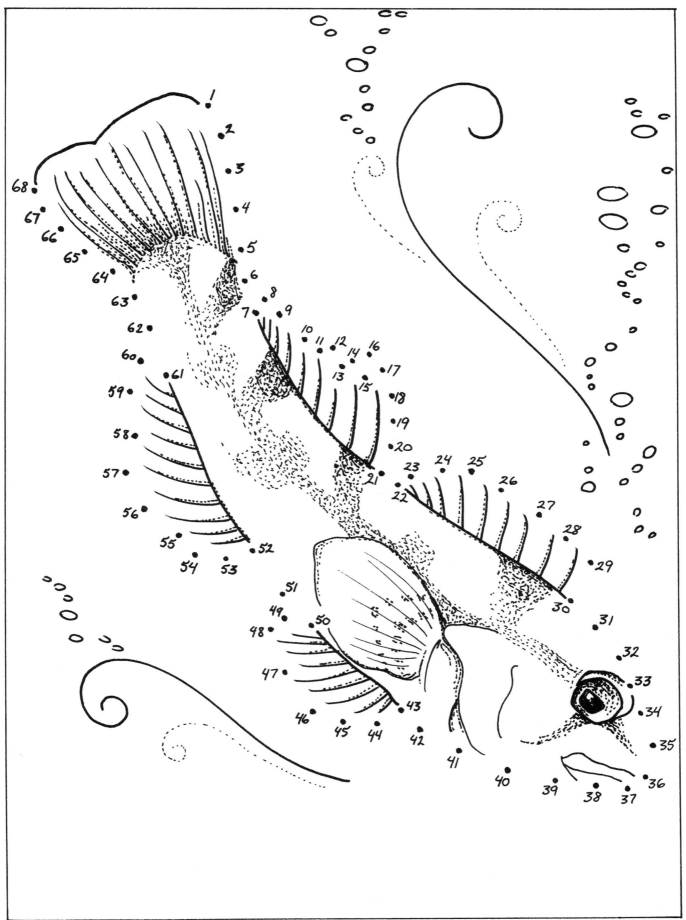

Name:	Snow Leopard
Size:	About 50 inches (125cm) long (not including the tail)
Where It Is Endangered:	Nepal (Central Asia)
Habitat:	Remote mountains

The Snow Leopard is a hunter, like other members of the cat family. It tracks and eats wild sheep, hare, and even domestic livestock like goats. Snow Leopards hunt for food at dawn or at dusk.

These beautiful leopards have been killed for their fur, but now it is illegal to kill them.

Scientists have trapped some Snow Leopards and attached collars with radio transmitters to them. Tracking by radio helps the scientists learn where the cats travel and how big their territory is.

Pale yellow-tan (nearly white), black circles and spots

Name:	Thick-Billed Parrot
Size:	About 15 inches (37.5cm) long
Where It Is Endangered:	Mexico
Habitat:	Pine and oak forests

These colorful long-tailed birds are rare because so many have been captured for sale as pets, and because the pine and oak forests where they live are being cut down. They have already become extinct in the United States.

Zoos and wildlife workers have been trying to breed this parrot in large aviaries. A small flock of Thick-Billed Parrots was released in Arizona in 1993, with the hopes of starting a new population in the United States.

Bright green body, red forehead, red shoulders, red leg feathers, dark grey beak, yellowish skin around the eyes

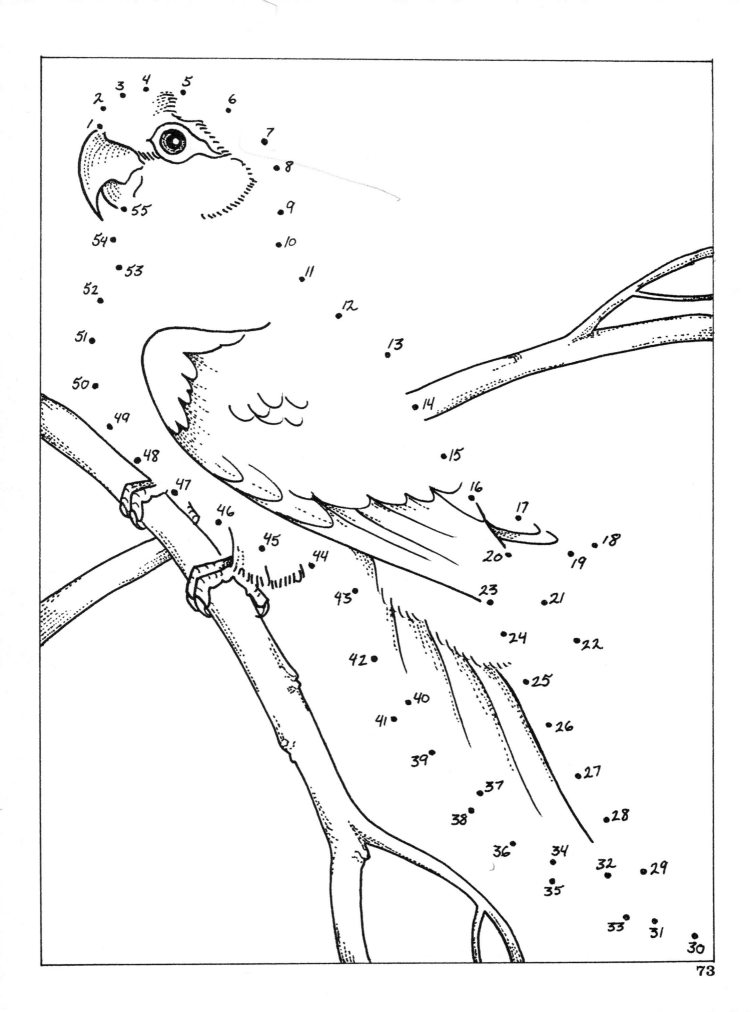

73

Name:	White Rhinoceros
Size:	About 5 to 6 feet (1.5—1.8m) high at the shoulder
Where It Is Endangered:	Africa
Habitat:	Open grassland and savannahs

This huge rhinoceros isn't really white, it's just lighter in color than other rhinos. All rhinos have thick, tough skin. They look hairless, but they have long, coarse hairs on their ears!

Rhinos are vegetarians, eating grass and other plants. Many have been killed by hunters for their big, valuable horns. The horns are used to make handles for daggers in the Mideast.

Some scientists think that only a few thousand White Rhinos are left. Other species of rhino are endangered too—the Black Rhino of Africa, and the Sumatran Rhino.

Light brownish grey

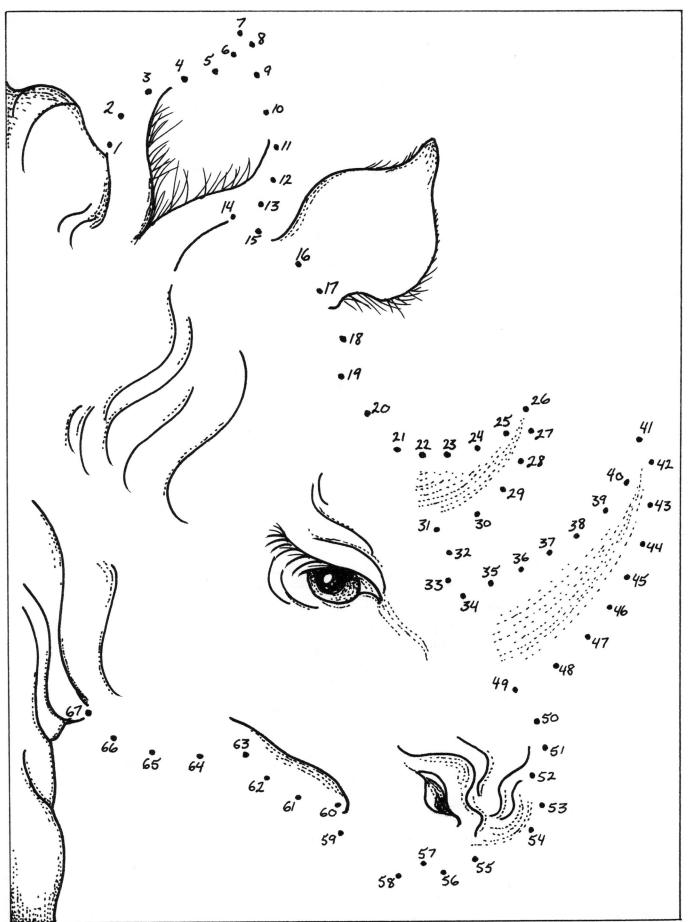

Name:	Whooping Crane
Size:	About 5 feet (1.5m) tall
Where It Is Endangered:	North America
Habitat:	Bogs, prairie pools, open marshy areas

The Whooping Crane is named for its loud trumpeting call. It has a long graceful neck, and long legs for wading in water. It is the tallest bird in North America!

The Whooper nests in wet open prairies in northwestern Canada, and migrates south to spend the winter in southern Texas. It is very close to becoming extinct.

Some Whooping Cranes have been shot by hunters, but scientists aren't sure why this bird has become so rare. Conservationists have hatched Whooping Crane eggs in captivity. Sandhill Cranes, a more common species, were used to hatch the Whoopers' eggs.

Snowy white body, red cap on head, black feathers on tip of wings

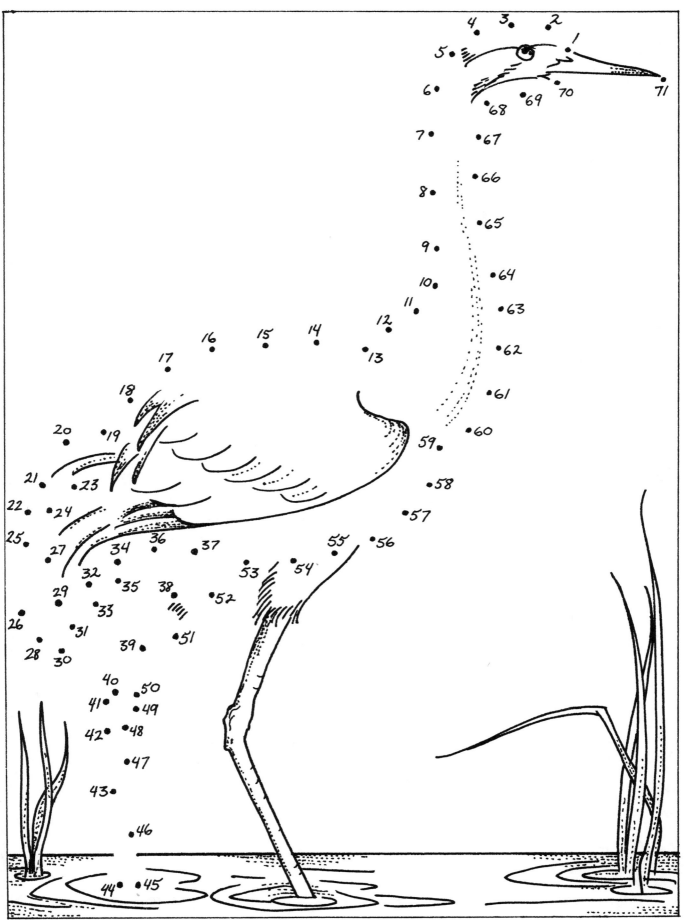

Name:	Yellow-Eyed Penguin
Size:	About 25 inches (62.5cm) tall
Where It Is Endangered:	New Zealand (South Island)
Habitat:	Cool, shady, sandy beaches

All species of penguin stand upright. They have short tails and webbed feet, and they can't fly because their wings are so tiny. Penguins use their wings like flippers when they swim underwater. They eat fish and shrimp.

Yellow-Eyed Penguins have become rare because the coastal forest trees in their nesting area have been cut to make open farmland. Also, ferrets and cats have destroyed many of the penguins' young chicks. Wildlife workers have tried to fence off the nesting sites so the chicks will be safe.

The eggs of the Yellow-Eyed Penguin hatch around November, the warm season in New Zealand.

Pale yellow eyes, yellow band on head, pink feet, pinkish orange beak, black back, white chest

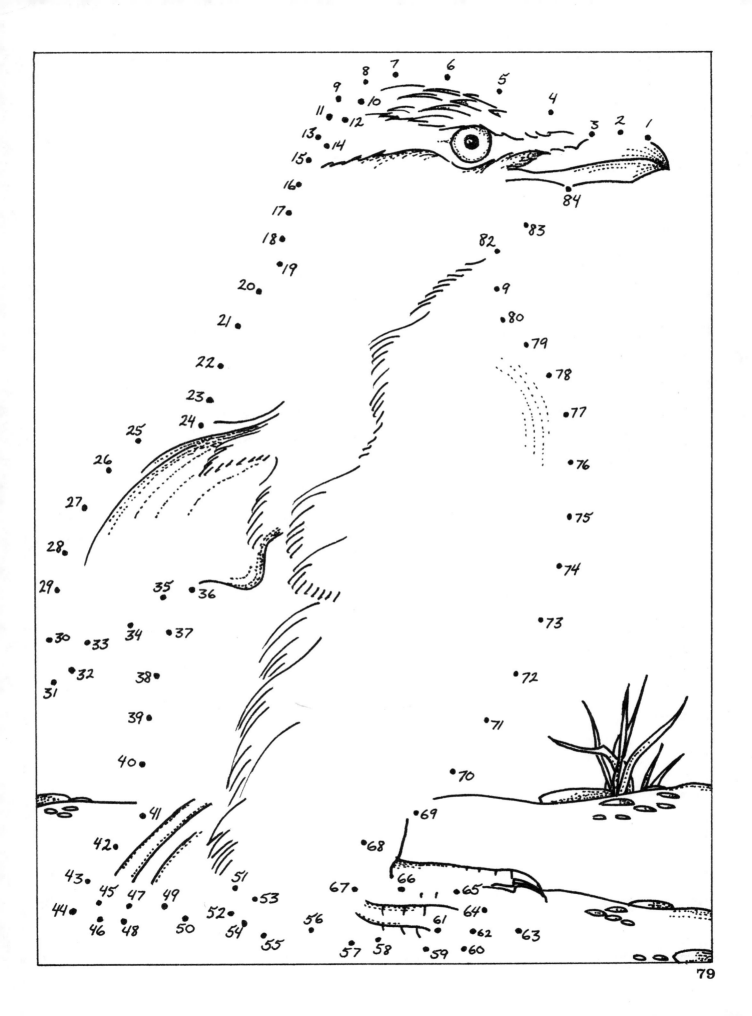

Contents/Index